PARIS

First published in the United States of America in 1999
by UNIVERSE PUBLISHING
A Division of Rizzoli International Publications, Inc.
300 Park Avenue South
New York, NY 10010

and

THE VENDOME PRESS

Front cover photograph: Notre-Dame. Photograph by Damien Lefèvre
Back cover photograph: Métro station entrance by Hector Guimard. Photo by Damien Lefèvre

ISBN: 0-7893-0379-5

Printed and bound in Italy

Library of Congress Card Number: 99-71288

99 00 01 02 / 10 9 8 7 6 5 4 3 2 1

UNIVERSE OF CITIES

PARIS

BY ALICE BIALESTOWSKI

PHOTOGRAPHS BY DAMIEN LEFÈVRE

UNIVERSE / VENDOME

more than any myth, Paris' power to fascinate remains undiminished over time. The City of Lights marries architecture, old and new, and captivates as much with its rich, incredibly diverse artistic heritage as with its history. The French capital's monuments are symbolic signposts in its collective memory, each reflecting a specific era and spirit contributing to the complex reality of an ever-developing whole.

The chronogical presentation of this volume provides the historical perspective necessary for an overall vision of Paris. Each building is placed in its immediate stylistic and historical context, while at the same time allowing the symbolic timelessness many of the sites and monuments have acquired over the years to be revealed.

A stroll through Paris is a journey through time. From Gallo-Roman Lutetia to medieval Paris, from the 17th century to the present day, the history of Paris is inscribed in its walls. For more than two thousand years, century after century, different styles and theories have modeled the city's evolution—an evolution inseparable from the city's political, economic, and social development. Paris' symbolically charged monumental vestiges form a stunning manual of architecture.

Saint-Germain-des-Prés church, boasting one of the oldest Romanesque bell towers in France, illustrates the influence of the Benedictines who contributed to making the Left Bank a place of cultural ferment. The construction of the Pont Neuf and the Place des Vosges reflects the vision of Henri IV, the capital's first urban planner.

Under Louis XIV, the Parisian landscape was transformed by the Hôtel des Invalides, the Place des Victoires, and the Place Vendôme. With Napoleon III and Baron Haussmann, the capital experienced an overwhelming urban revolution: the construction of broad avenues gave the city a new face, with the Opéra Garnier serving as its apotheosis. The Eiffel Tower, Gare d'Orsay, and Hector Guimard's Métro, all erected for the Paris World's Fairs, served as harbingers of modernity and the industrial age.

but Paris is not a static city resting on the historical greatness of the past. It had rejected the role of city-museum and continues to evolve, turning toward the future. Construction of the Grande Arche de la Défense, an extension of the historic axis formed by the Arc de Triomphe, the Avenue des Champs-Elysées, and the Arc de Triomphe du Carrousel—planned by the Sun King's landscape architect—is a perfect example of this movement. And, continuing the tradition of Notre-Dame, Place de la Concorde, and Sacré-Cœur, we now have the Centre Georges-Pompidou, the Pyramid of the Louvre and the new Bibliothèque de France.

Visitors quickly realize that Paris is also a living, breathing, multifaceted city. The world capital of fashion and luxury, it is a cosmopolitan crossroads attracting intellectuals and artists. From one bank of the Seine to the other, it amazes with the diversity of its moods and the variety of its neighborhoods. It beguiles the casual wanderer with unforgettable strolls along the river and surprise discoveries that reveal the very soul of the city.

For Paris is a city where losing oneself is recommended.

CONTENTS

"Fluctuat nec mergitur" (It floats yet sinketh not):
the motto for Paris formulated in the late 19th century,
officially approved by Prefect Haussmann, November 24, 1853.

ÉGLISE SAINT-GERMAIN-DES-PRÉS

At the heart of the legendary Saint-Germain-des-Prés quarter stands the oldest spired church in Paris. According to legend, in about 543 A.D., under the advice of Saint Germain, Bishop of Paris, Childebert I (son of Clovis) constructed a basilica and monastery dedicated to Saint Vincent and the Holy Cross. The final resting place of the Merovingian dynasty and of Saint Germain himself, the church became a Benedictine abbey in the 8th century, around the same time that the name "Saint Germain" was adopted. The sanctuary was remodeled and restored many times over. Following the destruction of the abbey in 1790, only the Romanesque church (rebuilt c. 1000), a portion of the abbatial palace, the remains of the cloister and a chapel dedicated to the Virgin remained. The church's bell tower, one of the oldest in France, was originally flanked by two additional towers, lending the church the nickname "the triple-bell tower church." The Gothic choir (12th century) is copied from Sens Cathedral. Vaulted in the 17th century, the nave is decorated with 19th-century murals executed by Hippolyte Flandrin.

Nearby, on the Boulevard Saint-Germain-des-Prés, the Café Flore, Café des Deux Magots, and Brasserie Lipp—famous institutions of postwar Paris—remain emblematic of this unique area.

Église Saint-Germain-des-Prés, Place Saint-Germain-des-Prés, 6th arrond., Métro Saint-Germain-des-Prés. Open daily from 8 am to 7 pm. Café de Flore (see page 46). **Café des Deux Magots,** *6 Place Saint-Germain-des-Prés (Tel: 01 45 48 55 25).* **Brasserie Lipp,** *151 Boulevard Saint-Germain-des-Prés (Tel: 01 45 48 53 91).*

CATHÉDRALE NOTRE-DAME

Symbol of medieval faith, the Cathédrale Notre-Dame exemplifies the magnificence of Gothic art. Begun in 1163 on orders from Bishop Maurice de Sully, construction on the site of a former 4th-century basilica was entrusted to an anonymous builder of genius, and completed in the first half of the 14th century. The project, the largest of the Middle Ages, brought together an impressive number of craftsmen of varied origins. Notre-Dame is inseparably linked with the history of France. The cathedral was restored by Eugène Viollet-le-Duc in the 19th century, and was the inspiration for Victor Hugo's famous novel, *The Hunchback of Notre-Dame* (1831).

Dominated by two tall towers and a 96-meter spire, the cathedral is an ingenious balance of vertical and horizontal lines. It boasts remarkable doorways and the famed Kings' Gallery, as well as architectural innovations like flying buttresses and magnificent gargoyles that serve as rain-spouts. In the 130 meter-long interior, the nave is flanked by double aisles lined with side-chapels. The Sacristy Treasury includes relics of the Passion, in addition to fine pieces of gold and silver plate. The cathedral is at its most impressive during high mass, when the play of light through the three large rose-windows combines with the music of the great organ.

It was around Notre-Dame that Paris' first schools, forerunners of the University, were established.

Cathédrale Notre-Dame, Parvis Notre-Dame, 4th arrond., Métro Cité. Open Mondays to Fridays from 8 am to 6:45 pm; Saturdays, Sundays, and holidays from 8 am to 7:45 pm. **Treasury:** *weekdays from 9:30 am to 6:30 pm (closed during religious holidays).* **Guided Tours** *(Tel: 01 44 32 16 70): April 1 through September 30, from 9:30 am to 7:30 pm; October 1 through March 31, from 10 am to 5 pm.* **High Mass:** *Saturdays, 6:30 pm; Sundays, 10 am, 11:30, and 6:30 pm.*

PONT NEUF

The Pont Neuf (New Bridge) is, paradoxically, the oldest bridge in Paris. Begun in 1578 under Henri III by Baptiste Androuet du Cerceau, and designed to facilitate the king's passage from one bank of the Seine to the other, it was inaugurated and baptized by Henri IV in 1607. This stone bridge (278 meters long, 28 meters wide), the first ever built without houses on it and the first with sidewalks, has always been extremely popular. It was a focus of bustling city life well into the 19th century, a daily open-air fair of traveling vendors and gypsies.

The Pont Neuf is made up of two sections connected by the tip of the Île de la Cité. Its twelve open arches are decorated with grotesque figures attributed to Germain Pilon. The candelabra, installed in 1854, is the work of Victor Baltard. In 1985 the Pont Neuf was "wrapped" by conceptual artist Christo, and in 1994 it was entirely covered in flowers by fashion designer Kenzo.

The square du Vert-Galant is dominated by an equestrian statue of Henri IV facing the magnificent Place Dauphine. At the end of the bridge, on the right bank, the department store La Samaritaine with its fine façade and monumental Art Deco sculptures (1926–28) rises from the Quai du Louvre. The store takes its name from the old "La Samaritaine" water fountain, the first in Paris, which once stood at the head of the bridge. The interior of the store features an interesting skylight and an admirable Art Nouveau wrought-iron staircase.

*Pont Neuf, 1st and 6th arrond. Métro Pont Neuf. **La Samaritaine**, 19 rue de la Monnaie, 1st arrond. Open daily except Sundays from 9:30 am to 7 pm, Thursdays from 9:30 am to 10 pm.*

PLACE DES VOSGES

An enlightened Henri IV is responsible for the construction of the Place Royale—renamed Place des Vosges in 1800—and the new life it brought to the Marais District. The new square was built on the site of the Hôtel des Tournelles, razed in 1563 by Catherine de Médici following the assassination of Henri II. Designed by an anonymous architect, the square was inaugurated in 1612 for the double wedding joining Louis XIII with Anne of Austria and Philippe IV of Spain with Elisabeth of France.

Place des Vosges is a perfectly symmetrical square courtyard surrounded by thirty-six identical arcaded houses. Their façades are a harmonious blend of white stone and red brick, topped by high, sloping blue-slate roofs. As the Place Royale, it was once the center of aristocratic life, a place of meetings and even duels, and the prestigious home of the likes of Madame de Sévigné, Cardinal Richelieu, and theologian and writer Jacques Bossuet. Later, Victor Hugo moved into the former Hôtel de Rohan-Guéménée, now the Musée Victor Hugo. An equestrian statue of Louis XIII, by Jean Pierre Cortot and Louis-Marie Dupaty, was erected in the center of the square in 1818.

A small passage leads directly to the Place des Vosges from the garden of the Hôtel de Sully (1624), one of the finest buildings in the Marais and currently used to house temporary exhibitions.

Place des Vosges, 3rd and 4th arrond., Métro Saint-Paul or Chemin-Vert. Musée Victor Hugo, 6 Place des Vosges (Tel: 01 42 72 10 16). Open daily except Mondays and holidays from 10 am to 5:40 pm. Hôtel de Sully (Caisse Nationale des Monuments Historiques et des Sites), 62 rue Saint-Antoine (Tel: 01 44 61 20 00). Open daily from 9 am to 6 pm, Fridays from 9 am to 5 pm.

PALAIS AND JARDIN
DU LUXEMBOURG

When Henri IV died, his widow, Florentine Marie de Médici purchased the property of François de Luxembourg for the construction of a vast Italianate palace, begun in 1615 by Salomon de Brosse. The stupendous edifice, inspired by the Pitti Palace in Florence and completed in 1622, is both Italian and French in style. It was decorated by the greatest contemporary artists, including Peter Paul Rubens, who painted the famous series of paintings entitled the *Life of Marie de Médici* now displayed at the Louvre. The palace was remodeled in the 19th century and today houses the French Senate and the Musée du Luxembourg (temporary exhibitions).

The gardens, also an amalgam of French and Italian styles, cover more than 50 acres. Their focal point is a large octagonal pool surrounded by raised balustraded terraces. Its model sailboats make it popular with children. Featuring a wealth of statuary and the Médici Fountain murmuring under the plane trees, the gardens have become a favorite with students of the Left Bank.

Nearby is the Place de l'Odéon with its famous theater, and the monumental Saint-Sulpice church, known for its Eugène Delacroix frescoes (Saint Anges chapel).

Jardin du Luxembourg, 6th arrond., RER Luxembourg. Open from sunrise to sunset. Guided Tour of French Senate (main entrance, 15 rue de Vaugirard) on request to the Caisse Nationale des Monuments Historiques (Tel: 01 44 61 21 69). Musée du Luxembourg, 19 rue de Vaugirard (Tel: 01 42 34 25 95). Open daily except Mondays from 11 am to 6 pm, Thursdays from 11 am to 8 pm. Théâtre de l'Odéon, 1 Place Paul Claudel (Tel: 01 44 41 36 36). Église Saint-Sulpice, 2 rue Palatine, Métro Saint-Sulpice or Mabillon. Open daily from 7:30 am to 7:30 pm.

JARDIN DES PLANTES

Commissioned of Jean Héroard and Guy de la Brosse by Louis XIII in 1626, the Royal Garden of Medicinal Plants became a major scientific institution under the direction of encyclopedist Georges Buffon (1739–1788) and the encouragement of illustrious scholars such as the Jussieu brothers and Daubenton. Transformed into the Musée national d'Histoire naturelle by the 1793 Revolutionary Convention, it was expanded during the 19th and 20th centuries with the addition of new galleries. Today the greenhouses, menagerie, maze, and remarkable alpine garden attract many visitors.

The museum—a kind of natural-science Louvre displaying the wonders of the organic, animal, and mineral worlds—is a source of endless discovery. The galleries of comparative anatomy and paleontology boast a fabulous collection of fossils, while the paleobotanical and mineralogy galleries display superb giant crystals. An immense skylight sets off some 120 specimens of different species against a spectacular backdrop in the Grande Galerie de l'Évolution.

Across the street from the Jardin des Plantes is the Paris Mosque, an ideal spot to relax over a steaming cup of mint tea. The Moorish architecture of the Mosque, like that of the Muslim Institute, dates from the 1920s.

Jardin des Plantes, main entrance Place Valhubert, 5th arround., Métro/RER Gare-d'Austerlitz, Jussieu or Monge. Open daily from sunrise to sunset. Menagerie open daily from 9 am to 5 pm. Musée national d'Histoire naturelle, 57 rue Cuvier (Tel: 01 40 79 30 00). Open daily except Tuesdays from 10 am to 5 pm. Grande Galerie de l'Évolution, open daily except Tuesdays from 10 am to 6 pm, Thursdays until 10 pm. Paris Mosque, Place du Puits-de-l'Ermite (Tel: 01 45 35 97 33). Open daily except Fridays and holidays from 9 am to 12 noon, and from 2 pm to 6 pm.

PALAIS ROYAL

Magically tucked away, the Palais Royal is second only to the Louvre as the largest and loveliest palatial ensemble in Paris. Commissioned by Richelieu in the 1630s, and then known as the Palais Cardinal, it became "royal" when Anne of Austria moved there with a young Louis XIV in 1643, and it continues to bear the mark of the Orléans dynasty, its owners from 1692 to 1848.

From the Cour de l'Horloge to the Cour d'Honneur, the building's present appearance dates from the Restoration and from the work by Pierre Fontaine, carried out under the reign of Louis Philippe (1830–48). The garden assumed its definitive shape in 1780 when the debt-burdened Duc de Chartres (later to become Philippe Égalité) had it surrounded with residences and shopping arcades designed by Victor Louis, though shady cafés and bawdy houses soon moved in. A mire of debauchery and a hotbed of rebellion during the Revolution, the Palais Royal and its charming shops are much more serene today. In 1986, the controversy over the installation of Daniel Buren's columns in the Cour d'Honneur reminded Parisians of this superb gem watched over by the ghosts of Colette and Jean Cocteau.

The Palais Royal, which has its own theater, is associated with the illustrious Comédie Française. On the rue de Beaujolais, the Grand Véfour restaurant still retains its original Restoration decor.

Palais Royal, Place du Palais Royal, 1st arrond., Métro Palais-Royal, Park open April 1 through May 31 from 7 am to 10:15 pm; June 1 through August 31 from 7 am to 11 pm; September 1 through 30 from 7 am to 9:30 pm; and October 1 through March 31 from 7:30 am to 10:30 pm. Théâtre du Palais Royal, 39 rue Montpensier (Tel: 01 42 97 59 81). Théâtre Français (Comédie Française), 1 Place Colette, 2nd arrond., (Tel: 01 44 58 15 15). Le Grand Véfour, 17 rue de Beaujolais (Tel: 01 42 96 56 27).

JARDIN DES TUILERIES

The Jardin des Tuileries owes its name to its clay soil, which until the 16th century was used for the manufacture of tiles (*tuiles*). This spot bordering the Seine between the Louvre and the Place de la Concorde is rich in history, and offers one of the most delightful places in the capital for a stroll. The gardens, which once surrounded a palace built over the old tileworks in 1564 by Catherine de Médici, were brilliantly redesigned in 1664 by landscape architect to the Sun King, André Le Nôtre, who installed two broad terraces and enlarged the central alleyway, creating the main axis for Paris' Triumphal Way.

This sumptuous French-style garden was one of the first in Europe opened to the public. From Antoine Coysevox's famous horses (originals in the Louvre) to Aristide Maillol's voluptuous bronzes, some one hundred statues ornament the garden. They are all the work of major artists and are representative of four centuries of sculpture. The garden was recently renovated and extended to the edge of the Louvre to include the Jardin and Arc du Carrousel.

Overlooking the Place de la Concorde, at the edge of the garden, stand the Second-Empire Orangerie, which houses the Walter Guillaume collection and Claude Monet's water lilies, and the Jeu de Paume, a temporary exhibition space devoted to contemporary art.

*Jardin des Tuileries, 1st arrond., Métro Concorde or Tuileries (Tel: 01 40 20 90 43). Open in winter from 7:30 am to 7:30 pm; in summer from 7 am to 9 pm. **Guided tours:** Wednesdays, Fridays, Saturdays, Sundays, and holidays at 3 pm (meet at the Arc de Triomphe du Carrousel). **Musée du Jeu de Paume,** 1 Place de la Concorde (Tel: 01 42 60 69 69), temporary exhibitions. **Musée de l'Orangerie,** Place de la Concorde (Tel: 01 42 97 48 16). Open daily except Tuesdays from 9 am to 8 pm, Mondays from 9 am to 9 pm. Closed for two years for construction work starting in August 1999.*

HÔTEL DES INVALIDES

Framing the far end of a sweeping esplanade leading to the Seine, the Hôtel des Invalides is a city within a city, containing a palace, convent, and military barracks. Louis XIV ordered its construction in 1670 to house army veterans wounded in his service. Completed in 1678, the edifice was designed by architects Libéral Bruant and his successor Jules Hardouin Mansart. It is reminiscent of the austere majesty of the 17th century with its monumental façade flanking the triumphal entrance. The buildings inside are strictly aligned along a symmetrical axis leading from the gateway through the royal court to the church. The double Saint-Louis-des-Invalides church, designed by Mansart and inaugurated in 1706, marks the apogee of religious art under Louis XIV. In 1989 the famous dome was completely regilded with 12.65 kilos of gold leaf. Under this dome lies the sumptuous red porphyry sarcophagus (1843) holding the ashes of Napoleon Bonaparte, transferred from Saint Helena in 1840.

The Hôtel des Invalides also houses the Musée des Plans-Reliefs (scale models of fortified cities and sites, antique maps, prints), and the Musée de l'Armée with its extraordinary collection of weapons. Nearby stands the Musée de l'Ordre de la Liberation, a memorial to the French patriots of the Liberation that gradually evolved into a museum of the Resistance, Deportation, and a free France.

Hôtel des Invalides (Tel: 01 44 42 37 67/72), entrance: Esplanade des Invalides, 7th arrond., Métro Latour-Maubourg, Invalides or Varenne. **Musée des Plans-Reliefs,** *open daily except December 25 and January 1 from 10 am to 12:30 pm and from 2 pm to 5 pm.* **Musée de l'Armée,** *open daily except November 1, December 25, and January 1 from 10 am to 5 pm.* **Musée de l'Ordre de la Liberation** *(Tel: 01 47 05 04 10), 51 bis Boulevard de Latour-Maubourg. Open daily except Sundays and holidays from 2 to 5 pm.*

PLACE DES VICTOIRES

The Place des Victoires, the first dedicated to Louis XIV, is the quintessential royal square. Designed to accommodate a triumphal statue of the king, commissioned in 1679 from sculptor Martin Desjardins following the victory of Nimègue, it owes its existence to the Duc de la Feuillade who was eager to express his admiration for the sovereign. In 1683 he purchased the Hôtel de la Ferté-Senneterre and then had it razed to make way for the square.

Designed by Jules Hardouin Mansart, the Place des Victoires was inaugurated in 1686. Its circular shape was an unprecedented innovation in urban planning. The streets running into it were designed so as not to face each other, thus making the statue of Louis XIV stand out against the façades of the buildings. Rue Étienne Marcel, laid out in 1883, opened up the square, which until then had remained relatively closed. The statue shows the monarch in all of his glory, mounted on horseback and raised on a pedestal surrounded by chained slaves and bas-reliefs of his reign's history. The monumental 12-meter-high bronze sculpture set the proportions of the site. The original statue was melted down during the French Revolution. The current statue of Louis XIV, installed under Louis XVIII, is the work of François-Joseph Bosio.

The rue des Petits-Champs leads off the square to the Galerie Vivienne and the Galerie Colbert, shopping arcades built between 1823 and 1826.

*Place des Victoires, 1st arrond., Métro Bourse. **Galerie Vivienne**, entrances: 6 rue Vivienne; 5 rue de la Banque; 4 rue des Petits-Champs. **Galerie Colbert**, 6 rue des Petits-Champs.*

PLACE VENDÔME

Place Vendôme is like a vast stage with the arcades of rue de Castiglione and rue de la Paix as a backdrop. Designed by Jules Hardouin Mansart late in the reign of Louis XIV, this architectural ensemble is one of the most successful examples of classic urban planning. The basic design developed by property speculators was taken up by Minister Louvois, who commissioned a seven-meter-high equestrian statue of the Sun King, ultimately melted down during the French Revolution.

What was originally a "royal square" took its present name from a townhouse owned by the Duc de Vendôme (son of Henri IV) that once stood on the site. Begun in 1687, it was modified in 1699 by the king, who rejected the initial square design for an octagonal one. Behind uniform façades completed in about 1720, wealthy connoisseurs (including the Scottish financier John Law and Mansart himself) built sumptuous townhouses. The column, cast from the melted-down bronze of cannons captured at Austerlitz, was erected in 1806 as a monument to the victorious Napoleonic armies. A statue of Emperor Napoleon by Antoine-Denis Chaudet (1810) was originally placed at its apex, removed in 1815, and finally replaced under Napoleon III by a copy. During the 1871 Paris Commune, the painter Gustave Courbet had the column and statue removed but the artist was later ordered by the courts to cover the costs of its restoration (1873).

Today the famous Ritz Hôtel, along with the most prestigious names in jewelry (Van Cleef & Arpels, Cartier, Boucheron, etc.) have made the Place Vendôme the ultimate in Parisian luxury.

Place Vendôme, 1st arrond., Métro Tuileries, Opéra, or Madeleine.

PALAIS DE L'ÉLYSÉE

The Palais de l'Élysée has been the official residence for presidents of the French Republic since 1873. This townhouse, built from 1718 to 1720 on orders from the Comte d'Evreux by architect Claude-Armand Mollet, remains one of the 18th century's finest. Acquired by Madame de Pompadour and then by the financier Beaujon, followed by the Duchesse de Bourbon, the building housed the National Printing Plant during the French Revolution, and became a public dance hall under the Directoire. Caroline Murat and Josephine would also take up residence, as would the emperor himself from 1808 until the end of the empire, and Prince Louis-Napoleon while preparing his coup d'état (December 2, 1851). The original Hôtel d'Evreux forms most of the current building's central section. New wings were added under the Second Empire.

Tapestries by Gobelin and 18th-century furnishings and paintings fill the palace's rooms. Especially noteworthy are the famous Pompadour, Doré, Argent, and Murat rooms. As a symbol of political power, the palace is protected by the presidential Garde Républicaine. Cabinet meetings are held there every Wednesday morning. Behind the palace is an English-style garden opening onto the Avenue Gabriel through a gate called the "Grille du coq" (1900).

Rue du Faubourg Saint-Honoré, which runs in front of the Élysée, is lined with magnificent townhouses and is home to international haute couture and luxury shopping (Lanvin, Chanel, Hermès, etc.).

Palais de l'Élysée, 55-57 rue du Faubourg Saint-Honoré, 8th arrond., Métro Miromesnil or Champs-Élysées-Clemenceau. Not open to the public.

MUSÉE RODIN

The Rodin museum, housed in the splendid 18th-century Hôtel Biron (named after Maréchal Biron, who owned it from 1753 to 1788) is one of those secret spots in Paris where time seems to stand still. The building, a masterpiece of stone constructed between 1727 and 1732 by Jean Aubert for financier Peyrenc de Moras, has all the hallmarks of a traditional Parisian townhouse. Auguste Rodin (1840–1917), its tenant from 1908 until his death, donated his collections to the State on condition that the house be made into a museum for his work.

A genius in tune with the artistic movements of his time, Auguste Rodin dominated sculpture in the late 19th and early 20th centuries. From his earliest to his most modern pieces, the museum offers a comprehensive look at the master's work: studies, marbles, bronzes, terra-cottas, watercolors, etc. The artist's impressive personal collections include sculptures by his pupil Camille Claudel as well as paintings by Claude Monet and Vincent Van Gogh. The wonders don't end with the charming house and its woodwork; outside a superb garden contains some of Rodin's most famous bronzes, such as *Les Bourgeois de Calais, Balzac, La Porte de l'Enfer* (Gates of Hell), and the famed *Penseur* (The Thinker).

Near the Rodin museum stands the Hôtel Matignon, residence of the French Prime Minister and the finest of all townhouses in the Faubourg Saint-Germain.

Musée Rodin, 77 rue de Varenne (Tel: 01 44 18 61 10), 7th arrond., Métro Varenne. Open daily except Mondays, 9:30 am to 4:45 pm in winter; 9:30 am to 5:45 pm in summer. Garden open 9:30 am to 5 pm in winter; 9:30 am to 6:45 pm in summer. Hôtel Matignon, 57 rue de Varenne. Not open to the public.

PLACE DE LA CONCORDE

The Place de la Concorde was originally laid out (by Jacques-Ange Gabriel) as the setting for an equestrian statue of Louis XV. Completed in 1772 it covers over 2.5 acres and is exceptional for its unobstructed views. Under the Revolution (when it was briefly renamed "Place de la Revolution") it was the scene of numerous beheadings. The guillotine was placed where the statue of Brest now stands (northeast corner), and both Louis XVI and Marie Antoinette were executed there.

In the center, the Luxor obelisk (22.86 metres high, approximately 230 tons in weight), presented to Louis-Philippe by Mehemet Ali in 1831, dates from the 8th century B.C. It is covered with hieroglyphics praising Ramses II and topped with a small bronze pyramid, recently regilded with two thousand sheets of gold leaf. Following the installation of the obelisk in 1835, Jacques-Ignace Hittorff (second of the two great designers responsible for the square) flanked the monolith with two fountains and placed statues representing the major cities of France on the eight pedestals built by his predecessor.

Inspired by the colonnade of the Louvre, Gabriel had two palaces placed at the nothern periphery of the square. These now house the French Naval Ministry and the Hôtel Crillon. Copies of Guillaume Coustou's famous *Marly Horses* guard the entrance to the Champs-Élysées (the restored originals have been in the Louvre since 1984).

Place de la Concorde, 8th arrond., Métro Concorde.

PANTHÉON

Standing on the crest of the Montagne Sainte-Geneviève, the Panthéon is one of France's most emblematic monuments. Begun in 1764, the structure was originally planned in fulfillment of a wish by Louis X, then critically ill, to rebuild the Abbey of Sainte-Geneviève. Jacques Germain Soufflot, the architect, attempted to combine Greek and Gothic styles. He did not live to see the completion of his work, which was carried out by the architect Rondelet. Topped by an ovoid dome that affords a superb view, the building is fronted by a monumental portico in imitation of the Pantheon in Rome. Its name means "dwelling of the gods." In 1791, shortly after it was completed, the edifice was transformed by the Constitutional Assembly into a republican temple for "receiving the ashes of great men associated with the era of French liberty." The church was definitively secularized in 1885, following Victor Hugo's funeral. Affirming the value of this republican memorial, the crypt now holds the remains of some sixty famous individuals, including Voltaire, Rousseau, Jean Jaurès, and André Malraux. The imposing, grandiose interior is decorated with frescoes by Puvis de Chavannes. The monument also houses a remarkable copy of Foucault's famous pendulum.

Next to the Pantheon stands the unusual Église Saint-Étienne-du-Mont, which houses the reliquary of Saint Geneviève, patron saint of Paris.

Panthéon, Place du Panthéon (Tel: 01 44 32 18 00), Métro Cardinal-Lemoine, RER Luxembourg. Open daily 10 am to 6:15 pm from April to September and 9:30 am to 6:30 pm from October to March. Église Saint-Étienne-du-Mont, Place Sainte-Geneviève (Tel: 01 43 54 11 79). Open daily 8 am to 12 noon and 2 pm to 7:15 pm, Sundays 9 am to 12 noon and 2:30 pm to 7:30 pm.

PONT DES ARTS

This footbridge links the Louvre area with the Faubourg Saint-Germain. Inspired by wooden bridges and the first wrought-iron bridge in France, this veritable prototype (nine arches) was erected on orders from Napoleon Bonaparte between 1802 and 1804 by engineer Louis-Alexandre Cessart. It takes its name from the "Palais des Arts," as the Louvre was known under the Empire.

The Pont des Arts was at first a toll bridge, but nevertheless attracted crowds of strollers intrigued by its unique decoration. Raised above the banks of the river, it initially resembled a hanging garden with bushes, flowers, and benches all lit by candelabras. The original bridge was demolished in 1981 because its fragile arches represented a hazard to river navigation. The steel reconstruction by architect Arretche is almost identical, though it has only seven arches. Overlooking the Île de la Cité, the new pedestrian bridge offers one of the finest views of the Seine. Equipped with benches and antique style street lamps, it is a favorite spot for artist and idle strollers.

Facing the bridge, in line with the Louvre's Cour Carrée, stands the graceful palace of the Institut de France (1663–91). Dominated by its stately cupola, it is home to five Academies, the most famous of which is the Académie Française (founded in 1635 by Richelieu).

Pont de Arts, *1st and 6th arrond., Métro Saint-Germain-des-Prés, Pont-Neuf, or Louvre-Rivoli.* **Palais de l'Institut de France,** *23 Quai de Conti, 6th arrond. Individual and group tours on written request to the Institut's secretariat only.*

CIMETIÈRE DU PÈRE LACHAISE

The Père Lachaise hill, where the former villages of Belleville, Ménilmontant, and Charonne once met, is one of the most unusual attractions in the French capital. Inaugurated in 1804 by Prefect Frochot, this cemetery occupies the site of the old Jesuit domain of Mont-Louis, made famous by a visit from Father de la Chaize, confessor to Louis XIV. Designed by Alexandre-Théodore Brongniart and reminiscent of an English garden, the cemetery is an ideal place for strolling and meditation. It forms one of the largest green spaces (over 100 acres) within the Paris city limits.

The famous and the forgotten lie side-by-side in this maze of extravagant funerary monuments: statuary in strange poses, weeping marble women, and monumental mausoleums. From the lyric to the grandiloquent, the sublime to the ridiculous, the range of 19th-century sculpture is exceptional.

In 1871, the 147 final hold-outs of the Paris-Commune federation were executed by a firing squad against a wall in the cemetery. The wall, now a memorial to the victims, has been named *Le Mur des Fédérés*.

Over one million people have been buried at Père Lachaise. Visitors make regular pilgrimages to the graves of Molière, La Fontaine, Balzac, Géricault, Chopin, Édith Piaf, and Jim Morrison.

*Cimetière du Père Lachaise, main entrance Boulevard de Ménilmontant (Tel: 01 43 70 70 33), 20th arrond., Métro Père-Lachaise. Open 8 am (8:30 am on Saturdays, 9 am on Sundays) to 6 pm (in summer) and 5:30 pm (in winter). **Guided Tours**, Tuesdays and Saturdays at 2:15 pm (meet at main entrance).*

ARC DE TRIOMPHE

The Arc de Triomphe, one of Paris's most recognizable monuments, rises from Place Charles-de-Gaulle-Étoile, so-named because of the twelve avenues leading off it like the points of a star. Construction of the arch, commissioned by Napoleon Bonaparte to commemorate his army's victories and designed by Jean-François Chalgrin, was begun in 1806 but not completed until 1836, under Louis-Philippe. Now considered a national symbol, the Arc de Triomphe crowns what is commonly referred to as the "most beautiful avenue in the world:" the Champs-Élysées.

The arch exemplifies the Empire in its combination of power, discipline, and extravagance. No fewer than 284 steps lead to the almost 50-meters-high observation deck where visitors enjoy one of the finest panoramic views of Paris. The monument displays the largest existing ensemble of early 19th-century sculptures illustrating the major events of the French Revolution and the Empire. The centerpiece is François Rude's masterpiece *Départ des Volontaires* (Departure of the Volunteers).

In 1840, Napoleon's ashes were laid under the Arc de Triomphe in a final tribute before being transferred to the Invalides, while in 1885, Victor Hugo was also given a posthumous tribute here. The tomb of the Unknown Soldier was lain beneath the arch in 1921. Since then, the flame of remembrance has been solemnly rekindled every day at 6:30 pm by war veterans.

Arc de Triomphe, Place Charles-de-Gaulle-Étoile, 8th arrond., Métro/RER Charles-de-Gaulle-Étoile. Arc de Triomphe Museum (Tel: 01 55 37 73 77). Open daily 10 am to 10:30 pm from October to March, and 9:30 am to 11 pm from April to September (elevator).

OPÉRA GARNIER

Place de l'Opéra is one of Paris' busiest intersections, where the great boulevards and the famed department stores of Boulevard Haussmann meet. The Palais Garnier was one of the major urban projects designed by Prefect Haussmann (others included public parks, sewers, and broad, straight avenues), whose ultimately political goal was to raze the old sections of Paris, which had been hotbeds of revolutionary activity, and thereby facilitate access by police and militia units. Architect Charles Garnier was an unknown when he won the competition to design the opera house. He worked on the building from 1862 to 1875, creating a new style unique to the reign of Napoleon III and reflecting the opulence of the Second Empire.

The main façade is ornamented with antique masks, busts of composers and allegorical groups symbolizing the arts, including a replica of Jean-Baptiste Carpeaux's *La Danse* executed by Paul Belmondo (the original is in the Musée d'Orsay). Surmounting the building's dome is a monument to Apollo sculpted by Aimé Miller. Inside, the main staircase and great foyer of colored marble form a spectacular polychrome ensemble. The Italianate red-and-gold theater contains 1900 seats. Repainted in 1964 by Marc Chagall, the colorful ceiling portrays famous ballets and operas.

The Palais Garnier, renamed Palais de la Danse following the inauguration of the Opéra Bastile in 1989, contains a library-museum and sponsors temporary exhibitions.

Palais Garnier, Place de l'Opéra, 9th arrond., Métro Opéra, RER Auber. **Tour and Lecture Department** *(Tel: 01 40 01 22 63).* **Opéra Library-Museum.** *Open daily 10 am to 5 pm. Guided Tours at 1 pm.*

CAFÉ DE FLORE

The Café de Flore owes its name to a statue of the Roman goddess of plenty that once stood over the entrance but has since disappeared. This café, a symbol of French intellectual life, opened at the end of the Second Empire and was acquired in 1939 by a man from the Aveyron region named Paul Boubal. For more than half a century, Boubal succeeded in perpetuating the cultural ferment of this favorite haunt of politicoes, artists, and intellectuals of all kinds.

The first writers to adopt the Flore were Joris-Karl Huysmans and Rémy de Gourmont. At the end of the 19th century Charles Maurras, founder of the magazine *L'Action Française*, wrote some of his articles for the early issues there. From Guillaume Apollinaire to Pablo Picasso, from Jacques Prévert to André Breton and Ernest Hemingway, the café's regulars have figured among the greatest artists of their time. The Flore is the cradle of existentialism, chosen in 1939 as headquarters by Jean-Paul Sartre and Simone de Beauvoir, who used it as their "office." Later, during the 1960s, the Flore began to attract luminaries from the theater.

Although the glory days of the Flore may lie in the past, celebrities still haunt its terrace. From the Art Deco ground floor to the British-style upper story, the café has retained all of its original character. With its neighbors, the Café des Deux Magots and the Brasserie Lipp, it represents the great era of Saint-Germain-des-Prés.

Café de Flore, 172 Boulevard Saint-Germain-des-Prés (Tel: 01 45 48 55 26), 6th arrond., Métro Saint-Germain-des-Prés. Open daily 7 am to 1:30 am. For the **Café des Deux Magots** *and* **Brasserie Lipp,** *see p. 8.*

BASILIQUE DU SACRÉ-CŒUR

Crowning the hill of Montmartre, the tall white silhouette of the Sacré-Cœur basilica is one of the major landmarks of the Parisian landscape. A France torn apart by the defeat of 1870 and the Commune set the political backdrop for the basilica's controversial construction, begun in 1877 under the direction of architect Paul Abadie. The edifice, entirely financed by private funds, was consecrated in 1919 and completed in 1923.

This romano-Byzantine monument is dominated by the cupolas of its dome and bell tower. Inside, a monumental mosaic by Luc-Olivier Merson ornaments the vault of the choir. The decor is designed as a symbolic representation of the history of devotion to the Sacred Heart, and extends to the side chapels and crypt. The basilica's bell, La Savoyarde, is one of the largest in the world, while the dome's summit affords a stunning view of Paris.

Montmartre, especially the Place du Tertre, with its crowds of painters and portraitists, has traditionally been associated with bohemian, artistic life. The Musée Montmartre, housed in the oldest building on the hill, evokes the turbulent history of this area of steep narrow streets, one of the last "villages" in Paris.

*Basilique du Sacré-Cœur, 35 rue du Chevalier-de-la-Barre (Tel: 01 53 41 89 00), 18th arrond., Métro Anvers, **Funicular**: departs from Place Suzanne-Valadon. **Basilica** open daily 6:45 pm to 10:30 pm. **Dome and Crypt** open daily 9 am to 6 pm from October to March, and 9 am to 7 pm from April to September. **Musée de Montmartre**, 12 rue Cortot (Tel: 01 46 06 61 11), Métro Lamarck-Caulincourt or Anvers. Open daily except Mondays, January 1, March 1, and December 25 from 11 am to 6 pm.*

EIFFEL TOWER

Omnipresent above the Parisian skyline, Gustave Eiffel's 300-meter-high tower is the most widely recognized symbol of the French capital. Built in less than two years as the centerpiece of the 1889 World's Fair, this stupendous technical feat was a triumph of the industrial age. Originally planned as a temporary installation, the "Iron Lady" caused an uproar when first erected. Only its usefulness as a radio transmitter saved it from the wrecker's ball. The tower's antenna has been broadcasting over 300 kilometers since 1906.

This huge steel construction weighs 7,000 tons and contains 15,000 components connected by 2.5 million rivets. Elevators (and stairs, for the athletic) lead to the three platforms open to the public. The highest platform houses the restored private apartments of Gustave Eiffel. The tower also has a brasserie, restaurants, and an audiovisual museum explaining its history. A beacon for aircraft was added in 1947, and television antennae in 1957. A new system of illumination, installed in 1986, highlights the design of this symbol of the new dawn of modernity, which has inspired artists and writers from Robert Delaunay to Guillaume Apollinaire.

The Champ-de-Mars, a former military parade ground and setting for Paris' World's Fairs, is a carpet of green running from the tower's base to the École Royale Militaire, founded by Louis XV in 1751. The Palais de Chaillot, built for the 1937 World's Fair, and the esplanade of the Trocadéro, both across the Seine, offer some of the finest views of the tower.

Eiffel Tower (Tel: 01 44 11 23 23), 7th arrond., RER Champ-de-Mars, Métro Bir-Hakeim or Trocadéro. Open 9 am to midnight from June 12 to end of August, and 9:30 am to 11 pm from September to June 11.

PONT ALEXANDRE III

The all-metal Alexandre III bridge, typical of the decorative art of the Third Republic, is an abiding model of elegance. Built for the 1900 World's Fair, it is named after the Russian tsar and celebrates Franco-Russian friendship. The bridge was designed by engineers Jean Résal and Amédée d'Alby, and features a single arch. The structure (109 meters long, 40 meters wide) was kept as low as possible so as not to obstruct the remarkable vista from the Invalides to the Champs-Élysées. Four magnificent gilded-bronze equestrian groups, by Pierre Granet, Emmanuel Fremiet, and Clément Steiner, and symbolizing Pegasus reined in by Glory, stand triumphantly at each of the bridge's four corners. On the Left Bank, the Glory of Warfare, on the Right Bank, Joy and Peace. Exuberantly sculpted motifs of marine flora and fauna and sumptuous candelabra complete what is surely one of the finest bridges in the world.

On the Avenue Winston Churchill, the Grand Palais and Petit Palais (1897–1900) typify turn-of-the-century establishment art. A mixture of genres is evident on the façade of the collectively designed Grand Palais, which accommodates prestigious temporary exhibitions as well as the Palais de la Découverte (a scientific and cultural center). The Petit Palais museum possesses a remarkable range of 19th-century paintings and exhibits the city's collections.

Pont Alexandre III, 7th and 8th arrond., Métro Champs-Élysées-Clemenceau or Invalides. Grand Palais, Avenue Winston-Churchill (Tel: 01 44 13 17 17). Open for temporary exhibitions. Palais de la Découverte, Avenue Franklin-Roosevelt (Tel: 01 40 74 81 73). Open daily except Mondays 9:30 am to 6 pm, Sundays and holidays 10 am to 7 pm. Petit Palais, Avenue Winston-Churchill (Tel: 01 42 65 12 73). Open daily except Mondays and holidays, 10 am to 5:40 pm.

MUSÉE D'ORSAY

In 1986, the old Gare d'Orsay became the missing link between the Louvre and the Centre Georges-Pompidou when it was converted from a train station to a vast museum devoted to the art of the second half of the 19th century and the early 20th century. Constructed by Victor Laloux at the request of the Orléans railway, the station and its hotel were inaugurated for the 1900 World's Fair. The façade, fronting an enormous metallic structure concealed beneath an envelope of stone, is ornamented with three sculptures representing the cities of Toulouse, Nantes, and Bordeaux.

When the rail lines were closed in 1939, the station barely escaped demolition. Its brilliantly executed conversion into a museum was decided in 1978. Under the direction of Gae Aulenti, architects Pierre Colboc, Renaud Bardou, and Jean-Pierre Philippon restored the immense nave and its skylight, installing delightful architectural detailing. The broad range of artistic creation on display (painting, sculpture, graphic arts, applied arts, architecture, photography, cinema) affords visitors an overview of the evolution of the era, and this in a setting emblematic of the industrial age.

Opposite the museum, the Hôtel de Salm-Kyrburg (1782–87), now the Musée de la Légion d'Honneur et des Ordres de la Chevalerie, is representative of the splendid 18th-century townhouses of the Faubourg Saint-Germain.

Musée d'Orsay, 1 rue de Bellechasse (Tel: 01 40 49 48 14), 7th arrond., Métro Solférino, RER Musée-d'Orsay. Open daily except Mondays 10 am to 6 pm, Thursdays to 9:45 pm. **Musée de la Légion d'Honneur et des Ordres de la Chevalerie,** *2 rue de Bellechasse (Tel: 01 40 62 84 25). Open daily except Mondays 11 am to 5 pm.*

HECTOR GUIMARD'S PARIS

As the man who spearheaded the Art Nouveau movement in France, Hector Guimard (1868–1942) was by far the most innovative architect of his time. Famous for his Paris Métro entrances, he also revolutionized the convention of bourgeois Parisian dwellings.

Designed at the request of the Paris Métropolitain for the 1900 World's Fair, Guimard's ornate subway entrances were initially ridiculed by the public. Inspired by the luxuriance of nature, these elegant structures display the inventiveness of the master, who designed a modular, standardized series adaptable to the requirements of each station. With daring virtuosity, he demonstrated the potential of wrought iron, seamlessly fusing technique and "Guimard style." The entrances to the Porte Dauphine and Place des Abesses Métro stations feature the last surviving skylights.

The Auteuil section of Paris, leading casual strollers back into turn-of-the-century Paris, contains the best of Guimard's work. Among the most stunning examples is the Castel Béranger, completed in 1898 and considered his masterpiece. Color and the variety of materials used are the outstanding features of this apartment-building façade ornamented with a strange bestiary. In a continuation of this spirit, Hector Guimard left his mark on much of the 16th arrondissement's urban landscape.

*Métro Porte Dauphine, Place du Maréchal-de-Lattre-de-Tassigny, 16th arrond., **Métro Abbesses,** Place des Abbesses, 18th arrond. **Notable Guimard buildings in the 16th arrond.:** Castel Béranger, 14 rue La Fontaine, Métro Jasmin; apartment buildings, 17, 19 and 21 rue La Fontaine; 8 and 10 rue Agar; 43 rue Gros; Trémois building, 11 rue François-Millet; Hotel Mezzara, 60 rue La Fontaine; Hôtel Guimard, 122 Avenue Mozart; apartment buildings, 18 rue Henri-Heine; 36 and 38 rue Greuze.*

GALERIES LAFAYETTE

The great department stores of Paris are tourist attractions in their own right, emblematic of the city's unique style. Their appearance in the capital under the Second Empire coincided with urban population growth and industrial expansion. The most popular by far are two flagship stores on the Boulevard Haussmann, Au Printemps and Galeries Lafayette.

Founded in 1895 by Théophile Bader and Alphonse Khan, the Galeries Lafayette began life as a small luxury goods shop. Constructed between 1906 and 1907 by Goerges Chedanne and expanded between 1910 and 1912 by Ferdinand Chanut, the store now occupies three buildings covering a total area of 120,000 square meters and is visited by an average of 500,000 people per week. A few traces of the Art Deco style are still visible on the façades, but the interest of the main building resides essentially in its magnificent hall surmounted by a glass cupola. The gracefully curved wrought-iron balustrades with their gilded relief-work are attributed to Louis Majorelle.

This temple of fashion keeps pace with the latest trends, presenting an extremely varied selection of work by couturiers and young designers. At Christmastime, animated scenes in the display-windows attract huge crowds.

The nearby rue Drouot, lined with shops selling antiques and rare stamps, is also home to the prestigious Hôtel Drouot auction rooms.

Galeries Lafayette, 40 Boulevard Haussmann (Tel: 01 42 82 30 25), 9th arrond., Métro Chaussée-d'Antin. Open daily except Sundays 9:30 am to 7 pm, Thursdays to 9 pm. Hôtel Drouot, 9 rue Drouot (Tel: 01 48 00 20 89), Métro Richelieu-Drouot. Open daily except Sundays 11 am to 6 pm. Auctions daily at 2 pm.

MUSÉE D'ART MODERNE
DE LA VILLE DE PARIS

The Palais de Tokyo, home to the city's prestigious museum of modern art, was constructed for the 1937 World's Fair. The architects were J.-C. Dondel, A. Aubert, M. Dastugue, and P. Viard.

The building, which boasts imposing sculpted-bronze doors, has two symmetrical wings linked by a colonnaded portico in white stone. Facing the Seine is a vast esplanade designed like a stone garden around a reflecting pool dominated by *La France*, a bronze statue by Antoine Bourdelle. The museum's collections cover a representative selection of 20th-century art, from Fauvism to contemporary installations. Especially distinctive among the major works on display are *La Danse*, by Henri Matisse, and Raoul Dufy's *La Fée Électricité*, one of the largest murals ever painted. The museum regularly schedules major temporary exhibitions.

Opposite stands the Palais Galliera (1878–94), a pastiche of the Italian Renaissance style, housing the Musée de la Mode et du Costume, the fashion and costume museum. Nearby is the Musée Guimet dedicated to Asian Art.

*Musée d'Art Moderne de la Ville de Paris, 11-13 Avenue du Président-Wilson (Tel: 01 53 67 40 00), 16th arrond., Métro Alma-Marceau or Iéna, RER Pont-de-l'Alma. Open Tuesdays to Fridays 10 am to 5:30 pm, Saturdays and Sundays 10 am to 6:45 pm. **Musée de la Mode et du Costume**, 10 Avenue Pierre-Ier-de-Serbie (Tel: 01 47 20 85 23), 16th arrond., Métro Alma-Marceau or Iéna, RER Pont-de-l'Alma. Open for temporary exhibitions daily except Mondays and holidays from 10 am to 6 pm. **Musée Guimet**, 6 Place d'Iéna (Tel: 01 45 05 00 98). Main museum closed for renovation until Spring 2000. **Galerie du Panthéon Bouddhique**, 19 Avenue d'Iéna, open daily except Tuesdays 9:45 am to 6 pm.*

BATEAUX-MOUCHES

The Seine, spanned by 36 bridges, is part and parcel of the french capital's history, landscape and soul. A center of urban activity until the 19th century, its banks were once home to a host of minor trades connected with navigation and waterways. Passenger boats have plied the Seine for centuries. In 1665, Colbert awarded letters of patent to the boatmen responsible for transporting the people of Paris. The first motorized river-buses made their appearance at the 1867 World's Fair. Built by shipyards located in the Mouche section of Lyon, they have been known as "Bateaux-Mouches" ever since. From 1880 until the turn of the century, these river omnibuses carried some 26 million passengers per year. However, faced with competition from the Métro, city buses and private cars, they ceased operation in 1934. Cruises for tourists began in the early 1950s. Today several companies operate boats from which tourists can view the monuments of Paris. After-dark cruises are especially enjoyable. Some companies have expanded their circuit to include the Canal Saint-Martin and the countryside bordering the Marne, land of the *guinguettes* or café/dance halls.

*Bateaux Parisiens Tour Eiffel, Port de La Bourdonnais (Tel: 01 44 11 33 44), Métro Trocadéro. Guided cruises (1 hour), daily 10 am to 9 pm. **Bateaux-Vedettes de Paris**, Port de Suffren, Métro Bir-Hakeim or Trocadéro, RER Champ-de-Mars. Guided cruises (1 hour), daily from 10 am. **Bateaux-Vedettes du Pont-Neuf**, Square du Vert-Galand (Tel: 01 53 00 98 98), Métro Louvre or Pont-Neuf. Cruises (45 minutes), daily at 10 am, 11:15 am, 12 noon, and every 45 minutes from 2 pm to 6:30 pm; "Paris by Night" cruises at 8 pm and 10 pm Mondays to Thursdays; 9 pm, 9:30 pm, 10 pm, and 10:30 pm Fridays to Sundays. **Canauxrama Canal Saint-Martin**, by reservation (Tel: 01 42 39 15 00). Cruises through Old Paris (3 hours), departures at 9:30 am and 2:45 pm. **Bassin de la Villette**, 13 Quai de la Loire, Métro Jaurès, departures at 9:45 am and 2:30 pm from Port de l'Arsenal opposite 50 Boulevard de la Bastille, Métro Bastille. **Les Bords de la Marne** (full-day cruise), departure at 8:45 am from Port de l'Arsenal.*

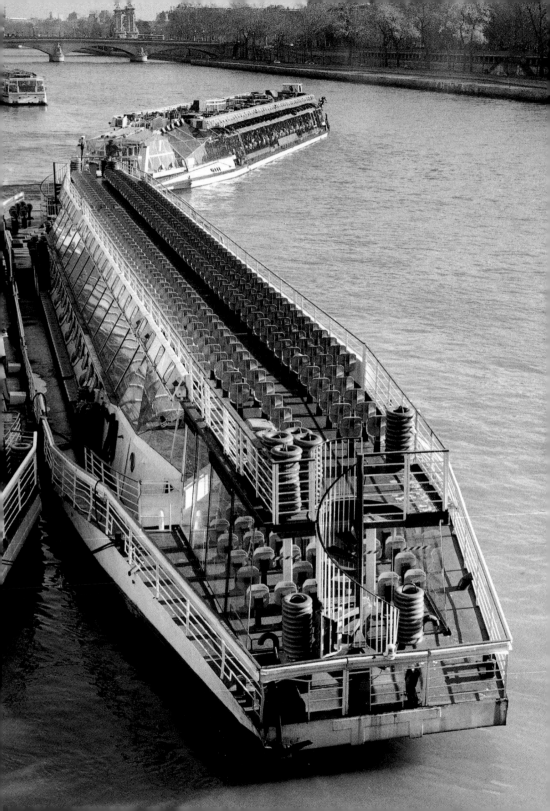

TOUR MONTPARNASSE

Rising 210 meters into the sky over Paris, the Montparnasse tower was built in the center of the 15th arrondissement from 1969 to 1973. The subject of keen controversy, it was designed by architects Eugène Beaudoin, Urbain Cassan, Louis de Hoym de Marien, and Jean Saubat.

Rising slightly to one side of the rue de Rennes, the steel and smoked-glass tower is oval in shape. Its foundation extends 70 meters underground. Equipped with 27 elevators, it has 58 floors, most of them occupied by offices. The top of the tower affords an exceptional view over a radius of some 50 kilometers on a clear day. The 56th floor has been turned into an air-conditioned observation deck containing exhibition rooms and a panoramic restaurant. The ground floor of the tower houses a bustling shopping center.

The Montparnasse section of Paris, a haunt of artists and intellectuals during the roaring Twenties, still boasts numerous artists' studios similar to the one once occupied by Antoine Bourdelle (1861–1929), now a museum. The famous brasseries Le Dôme and La Coupole, meeting places for the avant-garde, are now filled with a cosmopolitan crowd. A number of movie theaters round out the many attractions of the Boulevard Montparnasse.

Tour Montparnasse, entrance rue de l'Arrivée (Tel: 01 45 38 52 56), 15th arround., Métro Montparnasse-Bienvenüe. Open daily 9:30 am to 11:30 pm from April to September; 9:30 am to 10:30 pm from October to March; Fridays, Saturdays, and days preceding holidays 9:30 am to 11 pm. **Musée Bourdelle,** *18 rue Antoine Bourdelle (Tel: 01 49 54 73 73), Métro Falguière or Montparnasse-Bienvenüe. Open daily except Mondays and holidays 10 am to 5:40 pm.*

CENTRE NATIONAL
D'ART ET DE CULTURE
GEORGES-POMPIDOU

With eight million visitors annually, the Centre Georges-Pompidou ranks as one of the French capital's leading attractions. Much criticized following its completion in 1977, this vast center for cultural activity and the exhibition of contemporary art is a dramatic departure from the traditional museum. Industrial technology was the inspiration for its architects Renzo Piano and Richard Rogers. The building is a huge steel and glass parallelepiped 166 meters long, 60 meters wide and 42 meters high. Its functional components, all of them visible, are treated as an integral part of the design and are painted in red, green, yellow and blue. Inside, the Musée national d'Art moderne displays an expansive collection of 20th-century art.

The restored studio of Constantin Brancusi stands on the center's vast and always crowded esplanade. The adjacent Café Beaubourg was designed by Christian de Portzamparc. On the Place Igor Stravinsky (southern side of the Centre) a fountain by painter Niki de Saint-Phalle and sculptor Jean Tinguely serves as a striking contrast to the nearby Saint-Merri church.

Centre Georges-Pompidou, Place Georges-Pompidou (Tel: 01 44 78 12 33), 4th arrond., Métro Rambuteau or Hôtel-de-Ville, Métro/RER Châtelet-les-Halles. Renovation work scheduled until 2000; exhibitions from the Musée d'Art moderne, South Gallery. Constantin Brancusi Studio, Piazza, rue Rambuteau. Open daily except Tuesdays and May 1 from 12 noon to 10 pm; Saturdays, Sundays, and holidays from 10 am to 10 pm. Café Beaubourg, 43 rue Saint-Merri (Tel: 01 48 87 63 96). Église Saint-Merri, 76 rue de la Verrerie. Open daily 9 am to 7 pm.

CITÉ DES SCIENCES
ET DE L'INDUSTRIE

The vast La Villette park bordering the Ourq and Saint-Denis canals, on a site formerly occupied by the Paris slaughterhouses, is dedicated to the world of modern science and technology. The Cité des Sciences et de l'Industrie, a gigantic glass and steel parallelepiped designed by architect Adrien Fainsilber, opened in 1986. This polymorphous museum offers a spectacular range of exhibitions on the major scientific, technological, and industrial subjects of our time. Interactive displays, scale models, and games occupy the thematic modules of *Explora,* offering an instructive and entertaining approach to these disciplines. With its planetarium, giant aquarium, greenhouses and children's play area, the building hums with activity. A leading attraction is the *Géode,* a cinema boasting the largest wraparound screen in the world. Set over water, the sphere, measuring 36 meters in diameter, reflects the earth and sky on its silvery sides. The park, designed by Bernard Tschumi, is dotted with stunning red metal "follies." It is also home to the Grande Halle, one of the finest 19th-century ironwork structures in Paris; the Cité de la Musique (designed by Christian de Portzamparc); and the Zénith, a pop-music concert hall.

Cité des Sciences et de l'Industrie, 30 Avenue Corentin-Cariou (Tel: 01 40 05 80 00), 19th arrond., Métro Porte-de-la-Villette or Porte-de-Pantin. Open daily except Mondays 10 am to 6 pm. Sundays until 7 pm. **Cité de la Musique,** *221 Avenue Jean Jaurès (Tel: 01 44 84 44 84). Open daily except Mondays, Tuesdays, and Thursdays from 12 noon to 6 pm, Fridays and Saturdays from 12 noon to 7:30 pm, Sundays from 10 am to 6 pm.* **General Tour of Park** *(Tel: 01 40 03 75 64). From March 1 to October 31, Saturdays, Sundays, and Wednesdays at 3 pm (meet at the Information Folly adjacent to Métro Porte-de-Pantin).* **Zénith,** *221 Avenue Jean Jaurès.*

INSTITUT DU MONDE ARABE

The Institut du Monde Arabe, the fruit of an agreement made between France and twenty Arab countries, was inaugurated in 1987. Intended to present Muslim and Arabic civilizations and their relationship with other cultures, it was designed jointly by Jean Nouvel, Pierre Soria, Glibert Lézenès, and Architecture Studio.

Standing at the point where the Boulevard Saint-Germain meets the Seine, the IMA combines contemporary and traditional Arabic architecture in the heart of historic Paris. The curved, translucent façade facing the river contrasts with the severe rectangle of the main façade, a high-tech adaptation of the traditional *mushrabeyeh*, or wooden window lattices, in the form of a gigantic wall featuring panes of glass punctuated by 27,000 aluminum frames. The frames open and close automatically in response to the intensity of daylight, thus endlessly modifying the façade's pattern. Inside, the building contains meeting and study areas, a library, and a museum and exhibition galleries that are architectural attractions in themselves. Glass elevators lead to a panoramic restaurant and terrace. The remarkable exhibitions organized by the IMA afford an opportunity to explore the cultivated world of the Middle East within an outstanding contemporary architectural environment.

Passersby will also appreciate the contemporary sculptures lining the adjacent Quai Saint-Bernard.

*Institut du Monde Arabe, 1 rue des Fossés Saint Bernard (Tel: 01 40 51 38 38), 5th arrond., Métro Jussieu or Cardinal-Lemoine. Open daily except Mondays and May 1 from 10 am to 6 pm. **Lecture Tours**, Tuesdays through Fridays at 3 pm; Saturdays, Sundays, and holidays at 2 pm and 4 pm.*

LOUVRE

A medieval fortress erected in 1920 by King Philip Augustus, a fortified castle, and then the King's country residence under Charles V, the Louvre became an ongoing project for French monarchs from Henry IV to Napoleon III, who continually enlarged it. From the Old Louvre enclosing the Cour Carrée, to the most recent addition bordering the Esplanade du Carrousel, this royal palace is the largest ensemble of buildings in Paris. Over the years, the greatest architects, painters, and sculptors have contributed to the Louvre, designated a museum by the Revolutionary Convention of 1793.

In the center of this monumental group of buildings, known as the Grand Louvre following the renovation and extension work begun in 1981 and completed in 1993, rises the glass pyramid designed by architect I. M. Pei (1989). The pyramid covers the immense Hall Napoleon, affording direct access to the seven departments that make up the museum: Far Eastern, Egyptian, Greek and Roman Antiquities; Painting; Graphic Arts; Sculptures and Objets d'Art. The museum, considered one of the world's finest, is a maze of galleries filled with masterpieces including the *Winged Victory of Samothrace*, the *Mona Lisa* (Leonardo da Vinci) and *The Coronation of Napoleon* (Jacques-Louis David). Thematic or customized tours of this historic place help visitors to truly appreciate the universal heritage of art housed here.

Musée du Louvre, main entrance Cour Napoléon (Tel: 01 40 20 51 51), 1st arrond., Métro Palais-Royal. Open daily except Tuesdays 9 am to 5:45 pm; Wednesdays (museum) and Mondays (short tour) until 9:45 pm. **Tours, lectures, and workshops** *(Tel: 01 40 20 52 09).*

GRANDE ARCHE
DE LA DÉFENSE

The Grande Arche de la Défense is both a technical feat and a grand architectural statement, creating a new focal point on the historic Parisian axis leading from the Cour Carrée of the Louvre, through the Tuileries gardens to the Place de la Concorde and the Arc de Triomphe. Inaugurated in 1989, it is described by its creator, Denmark's Johan Otto von Spreskelsen, as a window on to the world.

The arch, a colossal streamlined hollow cube, is made of white marble. It is 110 meters high, 106 meters wide, weighs 300,000 tons and could easily accommodate Notre-Dame cathedral within its central opening. Its gigantic presence is lightened by a vast translucent structure—the "cloud"—hanging under its vaulted roof. Express elevators lead directly to the observation deck, which affords an unrivaled view of Paris. This functional building houses the French Ministry of Industrial Equipment, various multinational corporations and the Human Rights Foundation.

The Grande Arche is the final element of La Défense, a new business district dotted with futuristic towers begun in the late 1950s. Today, it has become a sort of "21st arrondissement" to the west of Paris. It is also a stunning open-air museum of contemporary art, containing sculptures and fountains designed by artists such as Alexander Calder and Joan Miró.

Grande Arche de la Défense, Parvis de la Défense, RER/Métro Grande-Arche. Open daily from 10 am to 7 pm.

BIBLIOTHÈQUE
NATIONALE DE FRANCE

The glass towers of the new French national library, rising above the Gare d'Austerlitz, create a new landmark on the Left Bank of the Seine. The design of the four towers, built on the initiative of the late French président François Mitterrand, has been the subject of lively controversy. The library was opened in 1996 and holds 12 million printed works formerly housed in the rue Richelieu's venerable but obsolete library.

The ambitious new library was designed by architect Dominique Perrault, who erected four towers, symbolizing open books, around a sunken garden. The library, a wealth of printed, audiovisual and electronic media, preserves a peerless heritage in terms of scope, variety and rarity. In an effort to be as comprehensive as possible, it provides free access to over 180,000 works and the latest in modern technology. It responds to the growing demand for information through an array of media that users can consult; these include microfilms, microfiches, and digitalized items. The catalog lists over seven million documents and is accessible via the Internet. The building also houses exhibition galleries and two auditoriums.

The varied landscape visible across the river from the library includes the Parc de Bercy memorial garden.

Bibliothèque Nationale de France, Quai François-Mauriac (Tel: 01 53 79 59 59), 13th arrond., Métro Quai-de-la-Gare or Bibliothèque-François-Mitterand. Open daily except Mondays: Tuesdays through Saturdays, 10 am to 7 pm; Sundays from 12 noon to 6 pm. Annual closing from September 2–15, inclusive. Internet address: www.bnf.fr.

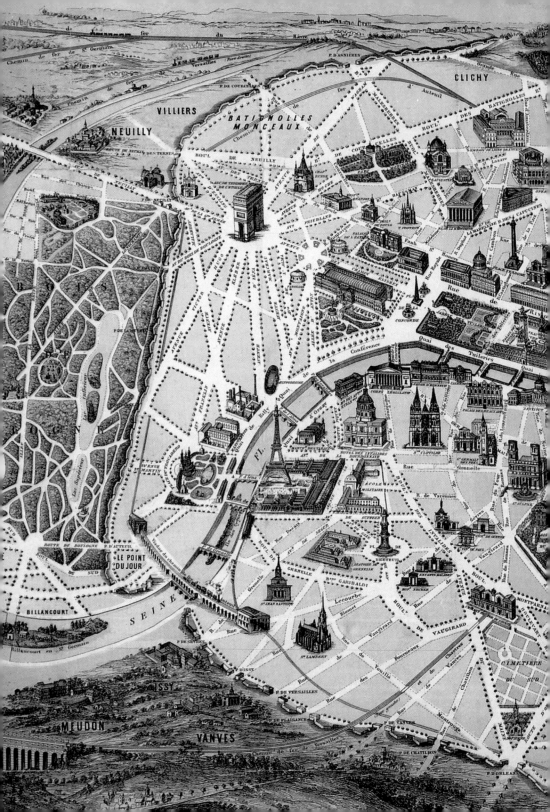